Copyright

Copyright © 2024 by SAI SAKETH CHERUKURI

All rights reserved.

No portion of this book may be reproduced in any form without written permission from the publisher or author except as permitted by U.S. copyright law.

Peri Ocular Insights

Unravelling Age and Gender Classification

Sai Saketh Cherukuri

A Deep Learning Approach

Sai Saketh Cherukuri
Introduction

Sai Saketh Cherukuri is a versatile individual with diverse interests and talents. His journey with the Tabla, a musical instrument, began in 2004, and since then, he has honed his skills, showcasing them through performances at a young age. Sai Saketh's mastery of Indian Classical music and his ability to connect with audiences through his Tabla performances reflect his dedication and passion for the art form.

On the sports front, Sai Saketh has been an avid football enthusiast throughout his life, representing his college team in his first year. His introduction to cricket during his schooling sparked a deep-seated passion, leading him to become an opening batsman and later play for the college team in his third year. His commitment, skill, and sportsmanship on the field make him a valuable team player.

In addition to his musical and sporting pursuits, Sai Saketh has a keen interest in technology. His hands-on experience building his Personal Computer and proficiency in soldering and working with circuitry highlight his technical prowess. During middle school, his involvement in the Science, Technology, Engineering, and Mathematics (STEM) club underscores his early pursuit of science, technology, engineering, and math.

Certified in AWS Certified Cloud Practitioner, AWS Certified Developer – Associate, AWS Certified Solutions Architect – Associate, and SAS Certified Associate: Programming Fundamentals Using SAS 9.4, Sai Saketh Cherukuri is a versatile individual poised to excel in any endeavor he chooses. His passion for music, sports, and technology and his commitment to excellence make him a standout talent with a bright future.

Dedication Page

I humbly dedicate this work to my Guru **Bhagawan, Sri Sathya Sai Baba.**

Abstract

Gender classification and age prediction have been fascinating challenges in computer vision, with wide-ranging implications and applications. Despite advancements, accurately predicting gender and age, especially in images with occlusions and distortions, remains a complex task, even for humans.

The COVID-19 pandemic added a new layer of complexity by necessitating face masks covering a significant portion of the face. This shift in behavior has underscored the importance of focusing on the periocular region—the area around the eyes—for facial recognition tasks, as it remains visible and can provide crucial data points for analysis. This contrasts with conventional methods that rely on the entire face, which may not be fully visible in many scenarios today.

Motivated by these challenges and the proven success of deep learning in computer vision, I implemented the "Peri Gender" model proposed by Husaain et al. Using PyTorch and convolutional neural networks, our model utilizes dense concepts within a residual framework, incorporating skip connections to enhance feature reuse across different scales. This design choice strengthens the model's ability to identify critical characteristics for gender classification.

To validate my method, I compared the performance of the "Peri Gender" model with established pre-trained models like ResNet-18, ResNet-34, and ResNet-50 on the UBIPr dataset. The results were promising, with the "Peri Gender" model achieving an impressive accuracy of

93.35%, surpassing the performance of the other models.

Building on this success, I extended the model to address age prediction, creating the "Peri Age" model. I trained the model on the FG-Net dataset by modifying the last fully connected layer to produce ten outputs. While the ResNet models achieved accuracies ranging from 58.03% to 60.34%, the "PeriAge" model achieved an accuracy of 50.00%, demonstrating its potential in age prediction tasks.

Combining the strengths of the "Peri Gender" and "Peri Age" models, I created the "Periocular" model, which achieved an accuracy of 32.29% on the UTK-face dataset. Interestingly, the model showed a higher accuracy in predicting female faces, suggesting that females exhibit more distinguishing features in the periocular region for gender classification.

The book represents a significant advancement in gender classification and age prediction in computer vision. Its innovative design, leveraging deep learning techniques, opens new avenues for improving facial recognition systems in challenging environments, benefiting various fields and industries.

Chapter 1: Introduction

The realm of age and gender recognition through periocular features presents a fascinating intersection of technology and human characteristics. This chapter delves into the complexity of this field, shedding light on the nuances and challenges it encompasses.

Chapter 2: Convolutional Neural Networks (CNN)

Central to understanding periocular age and gender recognition is grasping the architecture and workings of Convolutional Neural Networks (CNN). This section elucidates how CNNs extract features from data, emphasizing their pivotal role in this domain.

Chapter 3: Gender Classification of Periocular Images

Gender classification is a fundamental aspect of periocular recognition. Here, we discuss the data collection and preprocessing methods employed, along with developing the 'Peri Gender' custom model. The chapter also explores the integration of pre-trained ResNet models and compares their performance with those of these models.

Chapter 4: Age Prediction

Age prediction, while challenging, is crucial for comprehensive periocular recognition. This section details the data collection, preprocessing, and training processes, highlighting the utilization of ResNet and custom models. The chapter also addresses the inherent challenges in age prediction.

Chapter 5: Gender Classification on Video

Expanding the scope to video, this chapter elucidates the utilization of face detection in video frames for gender classification, showcasing the extension of face detection to this domain.

Chapter 6: The Model

In this chapter, I've explored how interactive interfaces are crucial in deploying machine learning models for real-world applications, making cutting-edge AI accessible to a broader audience. Effective interface design, blending aesthetics and functionality, enhances user experience with clear instructions and intuitive navigation. Visual cues like progress indicators aid interaction, while encapsulating model complexity simplifies user input and output from researchers to business analysts. Choosing the Gradio library for interface development highlights a focus on simplicity and versatility, ensuring a seamless user experience. Integrating interactive interfaces into model deployment workflows promotes accessibility and utility, driving innovation in artificial intelligence.

Chapter 7: Facial Recognition Technology

In this chapter, I discussed how facial recognition technology has evolved due to deep learning and computer vision. Techniques like facial feature extraction and CNNs are crucial. Despite applications in security, healthcare, retail, education, automotive, entertainment, marketing, and travel, challenges such as accuracy, bias, privacy, and ethics persist. Concerns include data protection, bias against demographic groups, and regulatory compliance (e.g., GDPR, CCPA). Future trends aim to improve accuracy, expand applications, and address ethical and privacy issues, emphasizing responsible use across industries.

Chapter 8: A Strategic Implementation Roadmap

This chapter will provide readers with a strategic roadmap for implementing "Periocular Insights: Unravelling Age and Gender Classification - A Deep Learning Approach" across industries. The roadmap details the methodology behind age and gender classification and discusses its advantages and disadvantages in each sector. By exploring this deep learning approach, readers will understand how advanced technology can address challenges and seize opportunities. This segment aims to equip readers with the information to implement age and gender classification effectively.

Chapter 9: References

The chapter provides a comprehensive list of references, citing relevant studies and papers that have contributed to the understanding and advancement of periocular age and gender recognition.

Chapter 10: Glossary

The section ends with a comprehensive list of glossary terms.

Contents

Forward 1

Chapter 1: Introduction 3
    Overview of Periocular Age and Gender Recognition .. 3
    Importance of the Study 4
    Scope and Objectives: 6

Chapter 2: Convolutional Neural Networks (CNN) ... 7
    Understanding CNN Architecture 7
    How CNN Learns Features from Data 8
    Relevance of CNN in Periocular Age and Gender Recognition 10

Chapter 3: Gender Classification of Periocular Images 12
    Data Collection and Preprocessing 13
    Creating the 'Peri Gender' Custom Model 14
        Using Pre-trained ResNet Models 14
        Training and Testing Process 15
        Performance Comparison with ResNet Models 15

Chapter 4: Age Prediction 17
    Data Collection and Preprocessing 17
        Outputting Age Ranges 18
        Training on ResNet Models and Custom Models 18
    Challenges in Age Prediction 20

Chapter 5: Gender Classification on Video 21
    Utilizing Face Detection in Video Frames 22
        Extending Face Detection to Gender Classification 23

Chapter 6: The Model 25
Peri Gender Code Snippet 25
Overview of 'Peri Gender' 26
Proposed Model 28
Chapter 7: Facial Recognition Technology 35
Facial Emotion Recognition 38
Techniques 38
Applications 38
Challenges 39
Facial Recognition in Security 39
Techniques 39
Applications 40
Challenges 40
Ethical and Legal Factors 41
Data Privacy 41
Bias and fairness 41
Regulatory compliance 42
Ethical considerations 42
Facial Recognition in Healthcare 43
Techniques 43
Applications 43
Challenges 44
Facial Recognition in Retail 44
Techniques 44
Applications 45
Challenges 45

- Facial Recognition in Education 46
  - Techniques 46
  - Applications 46
  - Challenges 47
- Facial Recognition in Automotive 48
  - Techniques 48
  - Applications 48
  - Challenges 49
- Facial Recognition in Entertainment 49
  - Techniques 49
  - Applications 50
  - Challenges 50
- Facial Recognition in Marketing 51
  - Techniques 51
  - Applications 51
  - Challenges 52
- Facial Recognition in Travel 52
  - Techniques 53
  - Applications 53
  - Challenges 54
- Facial Recognition and AI Ethics 54
  - Applications 55
  - Challenges 55
- Future Trends and Innovations 56
  - Techniques 56
  - Applications 56

Challenges 57
Conclusion 57
Chapter 8: A Strategic Implementation Roadmap .. 60
Conclusion 65
Summary of Findings and Insights 65
Limitations and Future Directions 66
Significance of Periocular Age and Gender Recognition 66
Chapter 9: References 68
Chapter 10: Glossary 72

List of Tables

Table 1: Results of the experiments 19
Table 2: Proposed model architecture. 29
Table 3: Pros and Cons of each field, ... 65

List of Figures

Figure 1: Various real-life situations that demand face occlusions. 4
Figure 2: Example of the periocular region: right eye image from the UBIPr dataset 5
Figure 3a: The Kernel being applied yields the topmost intermediate result for the activation map. 9
Figure 4: Typical Right eye female image, Augmented right eye female image 14
Figure 5: Confusion matrix of Peri Gender 16

Figure 6: Face detection using the Haar cascade classifier. 21
Figure 7: Code snippet of a residual block in 'Peri Gender' 25
Figure 8:Code snippet of a skip function in 'Peri Gender' 26
Figure 9:The architecture of 'Peri Gender' (a) The architecture of a residual block (b) The architecture of the residual group (c) The architecture of a skip module (d) The overall structure of the network architecture with four skip modules and four residual group. 29
Figure 10: Example outputs of the interface using an example image 33
Figure 11: 12 applications of facial recognition technology 37
Figure 12: 10 implications for further advancement... 60

Forward

Artificial intelligence (AI) is rapidly developing, and its intersection with social issues like gender recognition presents exciting possibilities and critical challenges. This book, authored by Sai Saketh Cherukuri, delves into this dynamic area, offering a fresh perspective at the forefront of deep learning research.

Sai Saketh's work is particularly noteworthy for its innovative approach. While some might view a student's perspective as lacking experience, Sai Saketh demonstrates the power of a curious and fearless mind. Unbound by conventional techniques, they explore new avenues of inquiry, challenging assumptions and sparking new ideas. Combined with a robust analytical foundation, this leads to insightful and thought-provoking exploration within the book.

Readers will embark on a detailed journey through the complexities of age and gender recognition using deep learning. Sai Saketh expertly guides them through the theoretical foundations of deep learning algorithms while addressing the ethical considerations surrounding their application in sensitive domains like gender and age.

This book goes beyond technical details, aiming to stimulate further exploration and critical discourse. It serves as a call to action for future scholars to push the boundaries of knowledge and ensure responsible development of AI technologies.

I commend Sai Saketh Cherukuri for his dedication, intellectual curiosity, and unwavering commitment to this crucial area of research. The impact of this work will undoubtedly extend beyond the academic community, shaping the future of AI thoughtfully and responsibly.

Dr. Darshan Gera

Associate Professor

Sri Sathya Sai Institute of Higher Learning,

Prasanthi Nilayam, Andhra Pradesh, India.

Chapter 1:Introduction

Embarking on a transformative exploration within the dynamic realm of computer vision, characterized by perpetual innovation, this book marks a pioneering foray into the specialized domain of Periocular Age and Gender Recognition. With an unwavering focus on the intricate facial subset encompassing the eyebrows and eyes, I aim to unravel the complex tapestry of interactions between facial features and the nuanced categorization of Age and Gender. The distinctive attention given to the periocular region propels this study to the forefront, aiming to decipher the subtle cues embedded within this often-neglected domain.

Overview of Periocular Age and Gender Recognition

Gender classification and age prediction have been topics of constant research and development in computer vision and have achieved relative success. They have various use cases and often provide solutions for many problems. Images of different levels of occlusions and distortions are found in the wild, making it challenging for humans to predict someone's Age and gender accurately. In the dynamic topography of computer vision, the pivotal focus of this book lies in unraveling the complexities of Periocular Age and Gender Recognition. Within this specialized niche, the study meticulously dissects the interactions within the periocular region— the often-overlooked facial subset containing the eyebrows and eyes. This pioneering exploration sheds light on the intricate dynamics underlying the categorization of Age and gender within this unique and nuanced domain.

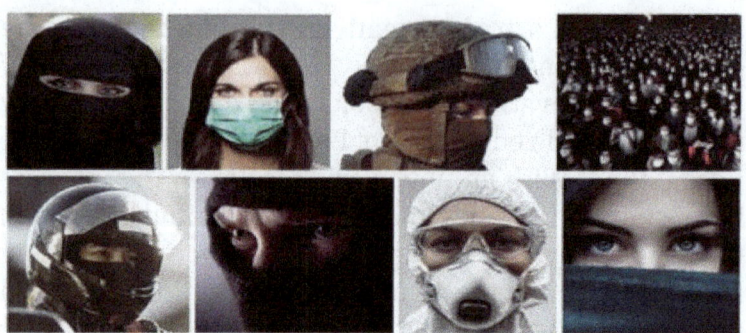

Figure 1: Various real-life situations that demand face occlusions.

Importance of the Study

Facial recognition software continues to be one of the most critical developments in the computer vision community, with a wide range of applications. Soft biometric traits, such as ethnicity, gender, and a rough age estimate, can be recognized by humans at first sight. While Age changes over time, race and gender remain permanent and don't change over time. Applications of facial recognition range from security, identification, marketing, advertisement, surveillance, and psychiatric studies to law enforcement.

Classical models have been developed and improved over the years, but they primarily rely on features of the entire face. When faced with a face covered with a mask or other occlusions, the performance of these models decreases. Due to the beginning of the COVID-19 pandemic, many people have been forced to wear masks. Classical methods employed by surveillance systems can decrease performance due to the partially or wholly occluded face, as shown in (Fig 1). For instance, many criminals wear a mask that fully covers their face, exposing only the periocular region for identification. The general public also covers their face when going to a dusty street, possibly due to religious beliefs and country-based laws.

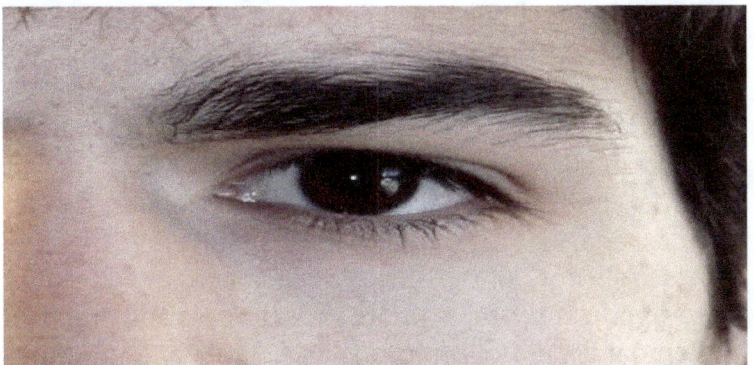

Figure 2: Example of the periocular region: right eye image from the UBIPr dataset

Thus, we cannot access other facial regions in such situations and have only the periocular region to identify from. This increases the difficulty, even for a human, in correctly classifying a person's gender and an accurate age range. GC using the iris is an invasive approach, and it is not socially acceptable or suitable for unconstrained scenarios. The periocular region outperforms the iris in the GC task. Due to facial and iris recognition limitations, an alternative method is the periocular region, the facial area surrounding the eyes (Fig. 2), which can be used as a cue for soft biometrics traits. Brown and Perrett reported that eyebrows and eyes together, eyebrows alone, and eyes alone are the top three facial areas that carry the most discriminative gender information.

Scope and Objectives:

The scope and objectives of this study extend far beyond the confines of academic inquiry. My aspirations encompass a comprehensive exploration that entails meticulous analysis of datasets and the integration of cutting-edge technologies. The primary objectives are multifaceted and ambitious: to cultivate robust models capable of discerning intricate patterns within periocular features, leverage the sophistication of Convolutional Neural Networks (CNNs) to their fullest potential, and, ultimately, apply these models in real-world scenarios. The culmination of my investigative efforts aims not only to enrich academic knowledge but, more significantly, to facilitate the seamless and practical implementation of periocular Age and Gender Recognition in diverse, dynamic settings.

This introduction serves as a deliberate Endeavor to set the stage for a profound and immersive exploration of the intricacies and implications of Periocular Age and Gender Recognition. The emphasis placed on the study's relevance and potential impact establishes a context for the reader, framing the subsequent chapters as a transformative journey into the forefront of cutting-edge research and technological advancement.

Chapter 2: Convolutional Neural Networks (CNN)

This chapter delves into the intricacies of Convolutional Neural Networks (CNNs), a cornerstone in contemporary deep learning methodologies. The narrative unfolds through a rigorous exploration of CNN architecture, elucidating how these networks discern and internalize features from data. Moreover, we scrutinize the profound relevance of CNNs in the specialized domain of Periocular Age and Gender Recognition.

Understanding CNN Architecture

Attempting to comprehend the behemoth of CNN can prove to be a daunting task. The science behind it is both complex and straightforward. We shall try to approach this carefully.

In Machine learning, a classifier assigns labels to data points, such as identifying objects in images. A convolutional neural network (CNN) is a particular type of classifier designed for image recognition. CNNs consist of 'layers' of interconnected Neurons, each with adjustable weights and biases. These networks recognize patterns in the data by systematically processing the input through multiple layers. Simply put, think of a classifier as a machine that looks at things and decides what they are. For example, it might look at a picture and say, "That's a cat!" or "That's a dog!". Picture a CNN as a bunch of layers, where each layer is like a 'filter.' These layers work together to understand the picture better and make a guess about its nature.

How CNN Learns Features from Data

There are a few key terms that are used to understand CNNs.

Tensors

Think of a Tensor simply as an n-dimensional matrix. It is a simple way to represent data in a structured format when dealing with pictures and multidimensional data. Let's say you have a grayscale image. Each pixel in the image can be denoted by a single number indicating its brightness. Now, if you have an N x N pixel image, you can create a tensor of size N xNn where each entry indicates the corresponding brightness of the picture. If its image has color, we create a three-dimensional matrix of width, height, and color channels (generally RGB).

Neuron

In the context of CNNs, a neuron is a fundamental computational unit that processes the information. It can be thought of as the biological neurons in our brains that process the information we receive through our senses. Each layer of a CNN has neuron(s) that process the data and pass it on to the next layer. The neuron takes in multiple inputs and passes a single output to the next layer.

Layer

A layer is a collection of neurons performing the same operation and having the same hyperparameters.

Kernels, weights, and biases

Kernels are small matrices that 'slide' across the image and detect features like edges or textures. Weights are parameters learned while training the model and determining the influence of the input pixels. Finally, biases are additional parameters added to the outputs to enhance the CNNs' learning and prediction capabilities.

As seen in the (figure 3a.) There is a kernel that 'slides' across the cup and creates a tensor of different color values. The size of the Kernel can be changed and is called a hyperparameter.

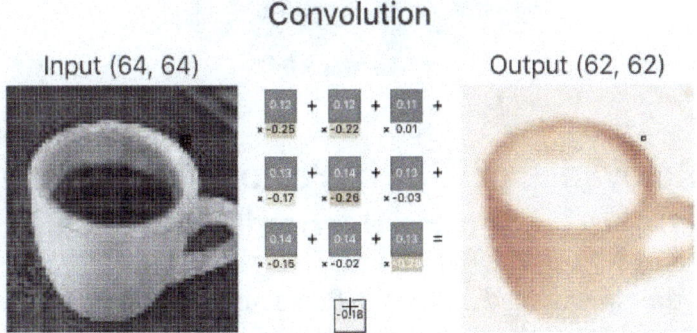

Figure 3a: The Kernel being applied yields the topmost intermediate result for the activation map.

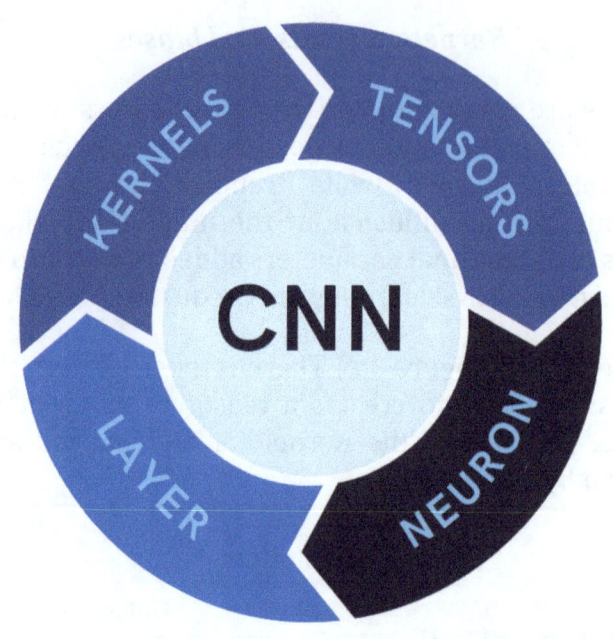

Relevance of CNN in Periocular Age and Gender Recognition

In the specialized realm of Periocular Age and Gender Recognition, the intrinsic capabilities of CNNs take center stage. Navigating nuanced intricacies, we delve into how these networks discern Age and gender-related features within the periocular domain. Establishing a direct link between CNNs and the unique characteristics of periocular regions, we underscore the indispensable relevance of CNN architectures in enhancing the precision and robustness of age and gender recognition systems. This section bridges the theoretical foundation of CNN architecture with the practical applications within Periocular Age and Gender Recognition.

This chapter represents an authoritative exploration into the core of CNNs, elucidating their architecture, unveiling the mechanics of feature learning, and establishing their pivotal role in advancing the frontiers of Periocular Age and Gender Recognition. The narrative is poised to equip readers with a profound understanding of the technological bedrock that underlies the subsequent analyses and applications presented in this comprehensive work. As readers journey through this chapter, they will gain insights into the transformative potential of CNNs in decoding the complexities of periocular features for Age and gender recognition.

Chapter 3: Gender Classification of Periocular Images

Gender classification (GC) continues to be one of the most critical areas of interest in face detection and computer vision problems solely because of its vast area of interdisciplinary applications. Since COVID-19, the push to obtain solutions to the issue of Masked facial recognition has increased drastically, as seen in. Due to masks being more prevalent now than ever, the need for GC has skyrocketed more than ever. A common issue faced in the area of GC is the unavoidable and natural occlusions in photos procured in the wild (unlike a controlled environment). However, as shown by Chandrashekar et al., the performance of GC on the periocular region performs well even when the iris is not visible because the corners of the eyes also contain distinguishing features.

Another interesting observation in the experiments by Chandrashekar et al. is the need for enhancing techniques to be used in the case of female periocular samples. The degradation in performance of the female subset may have happened due to possible make-up, eyebrow coloring, the use of glasses, and the presence of earrings. Most preexisting techniques imply a two-fold algorithm: first, they extract the facial features using landmarks and then pass them to a classifier model for predictions. The main downside of the previous models was that they were designed on custom rules and did not consider the nature of an image, thus requiring large amounts of time to evaluate effectively. Some techniques were trained on small CNN models and did not perform well on wild images. Given the exponential growth in facial recognition (FC) problems, particularly in CNNs and non-GC-related pattern recognition problems, they must be further explored and developed on periocular-related problems.

Data Collection and Preprocessing

As proposed by Hussain et al. [9], we first started with gathering the data sets required for completion. The UBIPr dataset was our project's best choice and primary dataset. The UBIPr dataset contains 10,252 RGB periocular images from 344 subjects in .bmp format with 501 × 401 pixels of image resolution. Images in this dataset were captured from a distance of 4 m to 8 m to include distance variability but in a controlled environment. This also contains metadata files for each image, which include coordinates of canthus points, the center of the iris, endpoints, and midpoints of the eyebrow, as well as information about gender, level of pigmentation angle of gaze, and various other landmark points. The dataset comes with an image and an annotated text file containing the labels for each image. The dataset contained more images of males than females, so data augmentation was done to balance the dataset. Random image solarization, random crop, random horizontal flip, and random invert were performed on the images for augmentation's sake, as seen in (Fig 4)

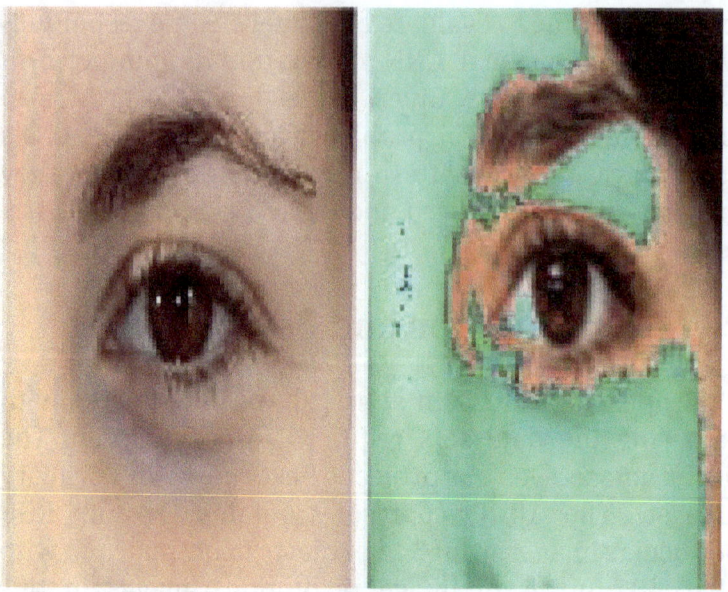

Figure 4: Typical Right eye female image, Augmented right eye female image

Creating the 'Peri Gender' Custom Model

Inspired by the results and the architectural framework provided by Hussain et al., I recreated the bespoke Peri Gender model. This custom-made approach represented a pivotal step towards achieving unparalleled accuracy in gender classification, underscoring the significance of a tailored model in capturing the subtleties of periocular gender cues.

Using Pre-trained ResNet Models

As described by Hussain et al., the ResNet-18 model was chosen as the backbone of the project due to its consistent performance in related fields. The pre-processed dataset was evaluated using three pre-trained models, ResNet-18, ResNet-34, and ResNet-50, thus creating a baseline for our Peri Gender model.

Training and Testing Process

A rigorous training and testing loop unfolded, marking a systematic passage of images through both the pre-trained ResNet models and the bespoke 'Peri Gender' architecture. This iterative process served as a crucible for the models, allowing them to discern intricate patterns within periocular features. The result was a refined understanding of gender classification, with each iteration contributing to the models' adaptability and precision. The pre-processed dataset was evaluated using three pre-trained models, namely ResNet-18, ResNet-34, and ResNet-50. The models were trained 25 times with a learning velocity of 0.01, momentum of 0.9, SGDM optimizer, ReLU activation function, and Cross Entropy Loss function. The training was performed on a Kaggle-provided CPU and a Tesla P100 GPU. Although BCE with Logits Loss is preferred for binary classification problems, the results obtained by Hussain et al. showed us that Cross Entropy Loss can work well. The results were as expected, with ResNet-50 outperforming its sister models. The accuracies achieved by ResNet-18, ResNet-34, and ResNet-50 were 91.89%, 91.48%, and 92.48%, respectively.

Performance Comparison with ResNet Models

To validate the efficacy of my tailored approach, a meticulous comparison was undertaken between the performance of the 'Peri Gender' custom model and the pre-trained ResNet models. The results revealed a commendable accuracy of 93.35%, aligning seamlessly with the benchmarks set by established models. This comparison underscored the efficacy and superiority of my tailored model in capturing the nuances of gender classification within the periocular context.

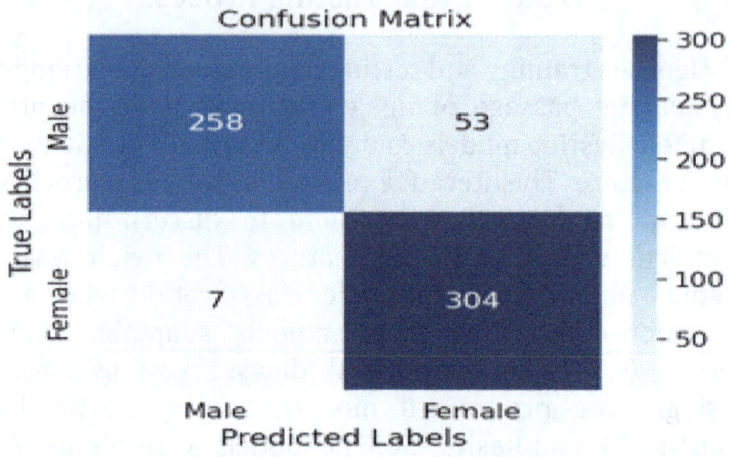

Figure 5: Confusion matrix of Peri Gender

Some things to note during this process were that ResNet-34 and ResNet-50 initially performed well due to their large number of layers, but their accuracy decreased over time as they learned various features from the dataset. ResNet-18 was chosen as the backbone for the model because it consistently learned the data compared to the other models. However, there were significant spikes and drops in accuracy when validating on the validation dataset (also UBIPr). This can be attributed to the data augmentation done on the dataset during preprocessing to obtain a balanced dataset. Another reason could be that the mini-batches may not be multiples of 64, meaning that the last batch may have less than 64 samples, leading to inconsistent data for the model to learn from. We can drop the previous collection, which is not a multiple 64, to address this issue.

Chapter 4: Age Prediction

In this chapter, we delve into age prediction within the periocular domain, exploring the challenges and modifications to model architecture. We detail the data collection process, utilizing the UT Face dataset for age annotations. We discuss the adaptation of output labels to represent age ranges and the training regimen involving ResNet models and our custom 'Peri Age' architecture. Despite strides, challenges like the lack of dedicated datasets and compromised image resolution persist. Through this exploration, we highlight the complexities of age prediction in the periocular context and the ongoing pursuit of accuracy.

Data Collection and Preprocessing

Navigating the intricate landscape of age prediction within the periocular domain, this section delves into the meticulous modifications applied to my model architecture to attain precision in predicting Age.

Collecting data for gender classification was straightforward due to the easy availability of the UBIPr dataset. The Data set included images with gender labels but did not include an age label. This made the process of gathering suitable data significantly harder. As a result, we decided to take advantage of the UTK Face dataset. The UTK Face dataset is a large-scale face dataset with a long age span (ranging from 0 to 116 years old). The dataset contains over 20,000 face images with annotations of Age, gender, and ethnicity. The photos cover considerable variation in pose, facial expression, illumination, occlusion, resolution, etc. This dataset could be used on various tasks, e.g., face uncovering, age estimation, age progression/regression, and landmark localization. As a result, we cropped the periocular region of the face and used it for Age prediction. The UTK Face dataset was meant for classical facial recognition models that employ the entire face. When we used it for our particular model, we resized it to crop only the periocular region. Still, due to the poor resolution of the images, further cropping resulted in loss of clarity, resulting in poor performance.

Outputting Age Ranges

A pivotal transformation unfolded in pursuing nuanced age prediction within the periocular domain. While The core architecture of the model remained the same, the final fully connected layer underwent a deliberate modification, transitioning from outputting two singular age labels to generating ten age ranges. This adaptive transformation aimed to provide a more realistic representation of the continuous spectrum of human aging. By embracing age ranges, the model sought to capture the inherent variability in facial features across diverse age groups, thereby ensuring a more comprehensive and nuanced prediction framework.

Training on ResNet Models and Custom Models

The augmentation of my model for age prediction mandated a rigorous and extensive training regimen. Preexisting ResNet models and the meticulously tailored 'Peri Age' architecture were subjected to a comprehensive dataset. This dataset was explicitly curated to accommodate the intricate patterns associated with age-related variations in periocular features. The dual-training approach was integral to a holistic exploration of the model's capacity to discern age-related cues. The fusion of established models with the bespoke 'Peri Age' model aimed at leveraging the strengths of both, resulting in a more robust and adaptable age prediction framework. As previously mentioned, the Peri Gender model architecture and the Peri Age model were largely the same. Still, for the Peri Age model, we replaced the last fully connected layer to have ten outputs instead of two to predict the ages of an individual from 0-100 divided into equal intervals of ten. However, just before the modified FC, we changed the Arg Max to SoftMax because we needed the probabilities of the different age intervals. We used the FG-Net dataset for training and testing and a dataset for age estimation and face recognition across ages consisting of 1,002 pictures of 82 people with an age collection from 0 to 69 and an age gap of up to 45 years. However, the results were not as good as the Peri Gender model. We trained and tested the same pre-trained models as before (ResNet-18, ResNet-34, and ResNet-50) but did not obtain satisfactory results this time. The accuracies obtained for ResNet-18, ResNet-34, ResNet-50, and our custom Peri Age model were 58.39%, 59.51%, 60.34%, and 50.00%, respectively.

Table 1: Results of the experiments.

	Dataset	ResNet-18	Custom Model	ResNet-34	ResNet-50
Gender	UBIPr	91.89%	**93.5%**	91.48%	92.48%
Age	FG-Net	53.89%	50.00%	59.51%	**60.34%**

Challenges in Age Prediction

Yet, the journey into age prediction within the periocular context encountered challenges. A significant hurdle surfaced due to the absence of a dedicated periocular dataset with pre-assigned age labels. A meticulous approach was adopted, involving manually cropping periocular regions from the UTK Face dataset. While indispensable, this compromise unavoidably led to a reduction in image resolution. This challenge underscores the critical need for comprehensive periocular datasets with pre-assigned age labels for more precise age estimation. This section offers a nuanced exploration of the intricacies involved in mitigating challenges on the quest for accurate age prediction within the unique confines of the periocular domain.

This section comprehensively explores the modifications made to models for age prediction within the periocular context. From the strategic adjustment of output labels to the dual training on established ResNet models and our custom 'Peri Age' model, the narrative unfolds the complexities and challenges inherent in predicting Age from periocular features. The poor resolution of the images directly affected the output of the model. The lack of easy availability of Periocular images with an age and gender label continues to be an issue in this field.

Chapter 5: Gender Classification on Video

Gender classification using video frames represents a dynamic and evolving area within computer vision, offering unique challenges and opportunities. The methodology typically begins with face detection algorithms applied to each frame, allowing for the identification and isolation of facial regions. This foundational step is crucial for subsequent gender classification, providing the necessary input data for analysis. Leveraging advanced techniques in face detection, such as Haar cascade classifiers or deep learning-based models, enables accurate detection of faces amidst varying poses, lighting conditions, and occlusions.

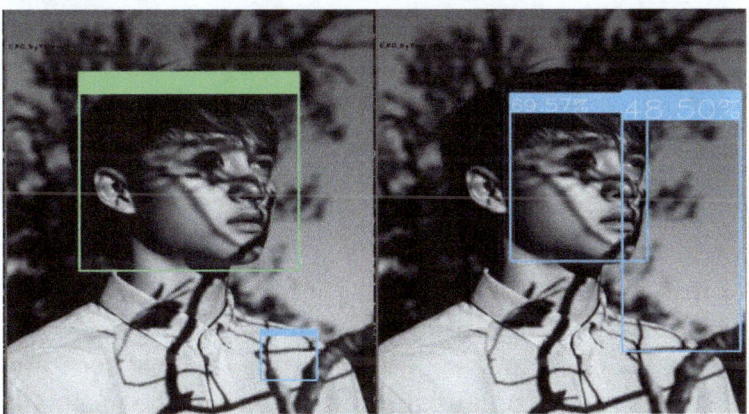

Figure 6: Face detection using the Haar cascade classifier.

Once facial regions are detected, the focus shifts to gender classification, where the goal is to determine the gender of individuals based on their facial features. This task often involves using pre-trained machine learning models, particularly convolutional neural networks (CNNs), trained on large datasets of labeled facial images. These models learn to extract discriminative features from facial images indicative of genders, such as facial structure, hair style, and other visual cues.

The process of gender classification within video frames extends beyond mere static analysis, as it encompasses the temporal dimension. This means that the algorithm must not only classify gender based on individual frames but also consider the evolution of gender attributes over time. Techniques such as frame-by-frame analysis, temporal aggregation, and motion-based features can be employed to capture the dynamic nature of gender expression within the video stream.

Real-time gender classification in video adds another layer of complexity, requiring efficient processing and analysis of frames as they are captured. This often involves optimizations for speed and scalability to ensure timely and accurate gender predictions, especially in applications such as surveillance, marketing, and human-computer interaction.

Utilizing Face Detection in Video Frames

At the core of our approach is the strategic utilization of advanced face detection algorithms applied to video frames. Each frame is subjected to meticulous scrutiny, treated as an individual image, with the primary objective of delineating facial contours accurately. Harnessing state-of-the-art face detection technology lays the groundwork for a more granular analysis of facial attributes within the temporal dimension. This intentional integration of face detection technologies into the temporal domain sets the stage for a nuanced exploration of dynamic facial characteristics over time.

Extending Face Detection to Gender Classification

Building upon the foundation of face detection, our methodology takes a transformative leap into real-time gender classification within video frames. Beyond the conventional delineation of facial features, our algorithm incorporates an additional layer of complexity, discerning gender attributes in real-time. This extension from mere face detection to gender classification introduces a novel dimension to understanding dynamic facial characteristics. The algorithm's ability to analyze gender attributes as they evolve within the temporal context represents a breakthrough, contributing to the evolution of gender classification methodologies.

The essence of this section lies in the seamless integration of face detection technologies into the temporal domain, offering a comprehensive exploration of gender classification within video frames. This transformative approach represents a synthesis of cutting-edge methodologies and technologies, propelling the field of computer vision into new frontiers of real-time gender analysis. By bridging the gap between static facial features and dynamic gender attributes, the chapter contributes to a deeper understanding of facial analysis in video streams, pushing the boundaries of real-time gender classification. The process of Gender recognition in a video using the custom Peri Gender model is not complex. It employs OpenCV for face detection and a pre-trained gender classification model, leveraging PyTorch. The code iterates over each video frame after loading the pre-trained model and setting up face detection using OpenCV's Haar cascade classifier. For each frame, it detects faces, preprocesses the detected face regions, and applies the gender classification model to predict the gender of each face. Bordering boxes are drawn around the detected faces, and the expected gender is annotated on the frame. Finally, the processed frames with annotations are displayed in real-time, providing visual feedback on the gender classification results.

Chapter 6: The Model

In the pioneering work by Hussain et al., Peri Gender architecture stands as a testament to innovation in periocular gender classification. Comprising four residual groups, each housing two residual blocks enriched with convolutional layers, batch normalization, and ReLU activation, this architecture embodies sophistication. What sets it apart is the seamless fusion of multiscale features through skip connections and depth concatenation layers, elevating feature representation to new heights. As the fused features converge, global average pooling marks a pivotal moment, paving the way for a fully connected layer with dual neurons poised to discern between male and female classes. This chapter unveils the intricacies of Peri Gender's design.

Peri Gender Code Snippet

```python
class ResBlock(nn.Module):
    def __init__(self, in_channels, out_channels, stride=1):
        super().__init__()
        self.conv1 = nn.Conv2d(in_channels, out_channels, kernel_size=3, stride=stride, padding=1, bias=False)
        self.bn1 = nn.BatchNorm2d(out_channels)
        self.relu = nn.ReLU(inplace=True)
        self.conv2 = nn.Conv2d(out_channels, out_channels, kernel_size=3, stride=1, padding=1, bias=False)
        self.bn2 = nn.BatchNorm2d(out_channels)

    def forward(self, x):

### The Residual block consists of :
# Conv_layer_1 ⟶ Batch_Normalization_1 ⟶ ReLU_activation_function_1
#     ⟶ Conv_layer_2 ⟶ Batch_Normalization_2 ⟶ ReLU_activation_function_2
```

Figure 7: Code snippet of a residual block in 'Peri Gender'

```python
class SkipConnection1 (nn.Module):
    def __init__(self, in_channels, out_channels):
        super(SkipConnection1, self).__init__()
        self.conv = nn.Conv2d(in_channels, out_channels=3, kernel_size=3, stride=1, padding=0)
        self.pool = nn.MaxPool2d(kernel_size=8, stride=8, padding=1)

    def forward(self, x):

        out = self.conv(x)
        out = self.pool(out)

        return out

# The skip connection function consists of simply 2 layers :
# Conv_layer ⟶ MaxPool_layer
```

Figure 8:Code snippet of a skip function in 'Peri Gender'

Overview of 'Peri Gender'

This model is a convolutional neural network designed for image classification tasks. It has several components commonly used in deep learning models: convolutional layers, batch normalization, ReLU activation functions, residual blocks, and skip connections. Here's an overview of each component:

1. ***Convolutional Layers***: These layers apply filters to input images to extract features. They have learnable parameters that determine their filter weights. This model has an initial convolutional layer with 64 output channels and a kernel size of 3x3. Additionally, each skip connection contains its convolutional layer, which changes the number of channels from the previous layer to match the desired output channels.

2. ***Batch Normalization***: This technique standardizes the activations across all dimensions of a mini-batch, allowing for faster training times and improved performance. Each residual block includes two sets of batch normalization after the convolutional layers.

3. ***ReLU Activation Function***: Rectified Linear Unit (ReLU) introduces non-linearity into the model by applying an elementwise threshold at zero. Any negative values become zero, while positive values remain unchanged. All activation functions in this model use the ReLU variant with 'in place' set to True, meaning intermediate results are directly modified instead of creating new tensors.

4. ***Residual Blocks***: A residual block skips one or more layers using shortcut connections, helping mitigate problems associated with vanishing gradients as networks grow deeper. Four residual blocks are stacked within the 'Res Block' class definition in this case.

5. ***Skip Connections***: These particular layers help propagate information through the network without transforming or preserving spatial information. There are multiple variations of skip connections defined in this code snippet, including different kernel sizes and strides.

6. ***Max Pooling Layers:*** These layers down sample feature maps by selecting the maximum value from overlapping subregions. Down sampling reduces computational complexity and helps prevent overfitting.

7. ***Concatenation Layer***: After processing the original input and various skip connections, they are combined via concatenation along the channel dimension. This allows the subsequent average pooling operation to consider features extracted throughout the network.

8. ***Average Pooling Layer:*** Average pooling computes the mean value within local regions, reducing dimensionality before passing data through fully connected layers.

9. ***Fully Connected Layer:*** At the end of the model, a fully connected layer with SoftMax activation performs binary classification based on the flattened output tensor from the average pooling layer. Dropout regularization is also applied here to improve generalizability.

Proposed Model

Peri Gender's architecture, as described by Hussain et al. [9], comprises four residual groups denoted as Res Gi (F, C), where i = 1,2,3,4. Each Res_Gi consists of two residual blocks denoted as Res_Bj (F, C), with j = 1,2, as depicted in Figure 4b. Each Res_Bj (F, C) includes a convolutional layer (conv), batch normalization (BN), and a ReLU layer, illustrated in Figure 4a. Multiscale features are fused after the first convolutional layer and each residual block, except the last one, by incorporating a skip connection Skip(F). Each Skip(F) comprises a 1×1 convolutional layer with three filters followed by an $F \times F$ max pooling layer (max pool) with stride F, as shown in Figure 4.

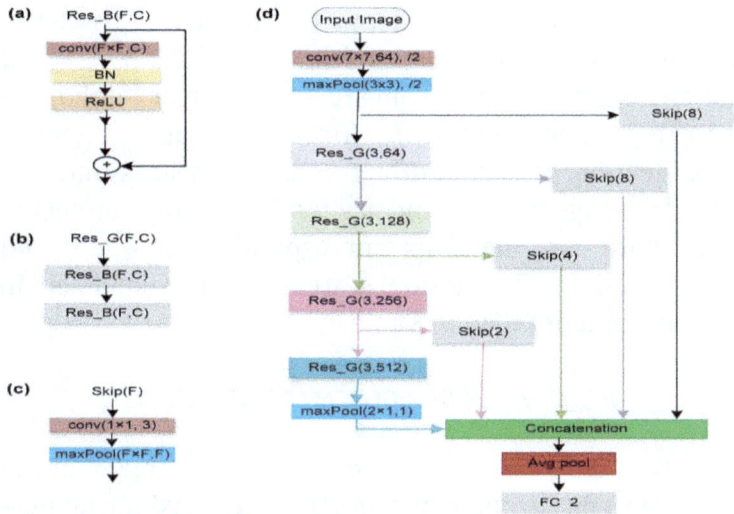

Figure 9 The architecture of 'Peri Gender' (a) The architecture of a residual block (b) The architecture of the residual group (c) The architecture of a skip module (d) The overall structure of the network architecture with four skip modules and four residual groups.

Table 2: The proposed model architecture

Layer name	Output size	Architecture
Image Input	$112 \times 224 \times 3$	
Convolution	$56 \times 112 \times 64$	7×7, 64, stride 2
Pool	$28 \times 56 \times 64$	3×3 max, stride 2
Skip Module (1)	$28 \times 56 \times 3$	1×1 conv, 3
	$3 \times 7 \times 3$	8×8 max, stride 8
Residual group (1)	$28 \times 56 \times 64$	$\begin{bmatrix} 3 & \times & 3, & 64 \\ 3 & \times & 3, & 64 \end{bmatrix} \times 2$
Skip Module (2)	$28 \times 56 \times 3$	1×1 conv, 3
	$3 \times 7 \times 3$	8×8 max, stride 8
Residual group (2)	$14 \times 28 \times 128$	$\begin{bmatrix} 3 & \times & 3, & 128 \\ 3 & \times & 3, & 128 \end{bmatrix} \times 2$
Skip Module (3)	$14 \times 28 \times 3$	1×1 conv, 3
	$3 \times 7 \times 3$	4×4 max, stride 4
Residual group (3)	$7 \times 14 \times 256$	$\begin{bmatrix} 3 & \times & 3, & 256 \\ 3 & \times & 3, & 256 \end{bmatrix} \times 2$
Skip Module (4)	$7 \times 14 \times 3$	1×1 conv, 3
	$3 \times 7 \times 3$	2×2 max, stride 2
Residual group (4)	$4 \times 7 \times 512$	$\begin{bmatrix} 3 & \times & 3, & 512 \\ 3 & \times & 3, & 512 \end{bmatrix} \times 2$
Pool	$3 \times 7 \times 512$	2×1 max, stride 1
Concatenation	$3 \times 7 \times 524$	Depth concatenation
Classification layer	$1 \times 1 \times 524$	Global Average Pool
	$1 \times 1 \times 2$	Fully connected, SoftMax

Table 2: Proposed model architecture.

Fusion of multiscale features involves a depth concatenation layer, resulting in a $3 \times 7 \times 524$ dimensionality. This concatenation layer enhances feature representation for periocular gender classification. Subsequently, the fused features undergo global average pooling and are fed into a fully connected layer with two neurons corresponding to male and female classes. The model's structure is visualized in Figure 4 and detailed in Table 1.

Model Architecture Interactions

Now that we've explored the fundamental elements of the Peri Gender model, it's worthwhile considering how these pieces work together. Initially, the model receives a reduced spatial representation derived from the input image, facilitating rapid extraction of meaningful features. Then, the sequence of residual stacks incrementally enriches these features, refining the model's discriminatory capabilities. Alongside the residual pathway, skip connections inject low-level cues into the hierarchy, balancing broad context with granular details.

Eventually, the concatenation stage merges information from all sources, yielding a holistic depiction amenable for downstream analysis. Adaptive average pooling compresses this global descriptor into a manageable vector, setting the stage for the FC layer and SoftMax activation to produce class membership estimates.

Overall, the Peri Gender model leverages sophisticated design principles and proven techniques drawn from deep learning research to construct an effective tool for addressing challenging image classification tasks. Its carefully crafted architecture ensures robustness against common pitfalls when scaling CNNs, ultimately delivering accurate and reliable performance.

Interactive Interface for Model Deployment

In machine learning and artificial intelligence, deploying models for real-world applications is as pivotal as their development. A significant aspect of this deployment is creating user-friendly interfaces that enable seamless interaction with the models. In this chapter, we explore constructing an interactive interface tailored to a pre-trained model, allowing users to harness its capabilities effortlessly.

The cornerstone of an effective interface lies in its ability to bridge the gap between complex machine-learning algorithms and end-users with varying levels of technical expertise. A harmonious fusion of aesthetics and functionality is imperative to ensure user engagement and satisfaction. The design process entails meticulous consideration of layout, color scheme, typography, and interactive elements to cultivate an intuitive and visually compelling interface.

Clear and concise instructions and well-defined input fields and output displays facilitate smooth navigation and enhance user experience. Visual cues, such as progress indicators and error messages, guide users through interaction, minimizing confusion and frustration.

Functionality: Empowering Users with Predictive Capabilities

At the heart of the interface lies its ability to encapsulate the functionality of the deployed model, providing users with a platform to harness its predictive prowess effortlessly. Whether the task at hand involves text classification, image recognition, sentiment analysis, or language translation, the interface serves as a conduit for users to input their data or queries and receive model predictions in real-time.

By abstracting away the intricacies of model architecture and implementation details, the interface empowers users across diverse domains to leverage state-of-the-art machine learning capabilities without needing specialized knowledge or technical expertise. The interface caters to a broad spectrum of users, democratizing access to cutting-edge AI technologies, from researchers and data scientists to business analysts and educators. The interface was developed using the Gradio library, a versatile tool that simplifies the creation of interactive machine-learning applications. Leveraging Gradio's intuitive interface-building capabilities, users can effortlessly input data and receive model predictions in real-time. This choice streamlines the development

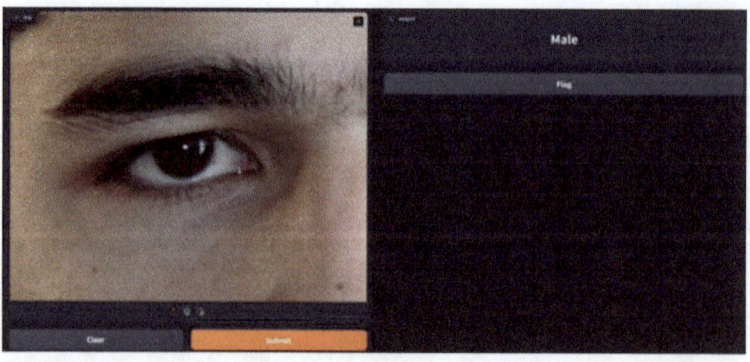

process and ensures a seamless and engaging user experience, enabling broader access to the model's functionality across various domains.

Figure 10: Example outputs of the interface using an example image

Conclusion

In this chapter, we've explored the pivotal role of interactive interfaces in deploying machine learning models for real-world applications. By bridging the gap between complex algorithms and end-users, these interfaces democratize access to cutting-edge AI technologies, empowering individuals across diverse domains to effortlessly leverage the predictive capabilities of pre-trained models.

A harmonious fusion of aesthetics and functionality lies at the heart of an effective interface design. Clear instructions, well-defined input fields, and intuitive navigation pathways enhance user experience, fostering engagement and satisfaction. Leveraging visual cues such as progress indicators and error messages facilitates seamless interaction, minimizing confusion and frustration.

Central to the interface's functionality is its ability to encapsulate the predictive prowess of the deployed model. By abstracting away technical complexities, users can effortlessly input data and receive real-time predictions, spanning tasks from text classification to image recognition and beyond. This democratization of access to state-of-the-art machine learning capabilities transcends traditional boundaries, catering to a broad spectrum of users, from researchers and data scientists to business analysts and educators.

The choice of the Gradio library for interface development underscores a commitment to simplicity and versatility. By streamlining the interface-building process, Gradio ensures a seamless and engaging user experience, facilitating broader access to the model's functionality across various domains. By integrating interactive interfaces into model deployment workflows, we pave the way for enhanced accessibility and utility, driving innovation and progress in the ever-evolving landscape of artificial intelligence.

Chapter 7: Facial Recognition Technology

Facial recognition technology stands at the forefront of innovation, offering transformative solutions across various industries and applications. In this comprehensive chapter, we journeyed through the multifaceted landscape of facial recognition, exploring its diverse applications, nuanced techniques, and pressing challenges. From enhancing security and healthcare to revolutionizing retail and entertainment, facial recognition's impact reverberates across various domains, reshaping how we interact with technology and each other. Delving into each area, we unravel the intricate techniques underpinning facial recognition systems, examine their real-world applications, and confront the ethical and legal considerations accompanying their proliferation. As we navigate through the intricacies of facial recognition, we uncover its immense potential and the imperative of responsible implementation and ethical stewardship in harnessing its power for the betterment of society. To enhance the understanding and application of facial recognition technology. Here are some areas where it can be applied:

1. **Facial Emotion Recognition**: Explore the use of deep learning for recognizing emotions from facial expressions, including techniques, applications, and challenges.

2. **Facial Recognition in Security**: Discuss using facial recognition for access control, surveillance, and forensic analysis, including case studies and best practices.

3. **Ethical and Legal Considerations**: Examine the moral implications of facial recognition technology, including privacy concerns, bias, and regulatory compliance.

4. **Facial Recognition in Healthcare**: Explore how facial recognition is used for patient identification, monitoring, and personalized treatment.

5. **Facial Recognition in Retail**: Discuss the applications of facial recognition in retail, such as customer profiling, personalized marketing, and fraud detection.

6. **Facial Recognition in Education**: Explore how facial recognition is used for student identification, attendance tracking, and personalized learning.

7. **Facial Recognition in Automotive**: Discuss using facial recognition in automotive for driver monitoring, personalized driving experiences, and vehicle security.

8. **Facial Recognition in Entertainment**: Explore how facial recognition is used for content recommendation, audience analysis, and user engagement.

9. **Facial Recognition in Marketing**: Discuss the applications of facial recognition in marketing, such as customer segmentation, targeted advertising, and campaign analysis.

10. *Facial Recognition in Travel*: Explore how facial recognition is used in the travel industry for customer profiling, personalized services, and security.

11. *Facial Recognition and AI Ethics*: Discuss the ethical considerations of facial recognition technology, including bias, privacy, and accountability.

12. *Future Trends and Innovations*: Explore emerging trends and innovations in facial recognition technology, such as 3D facial recognition, deepfake detection, and emotion-aware AI.

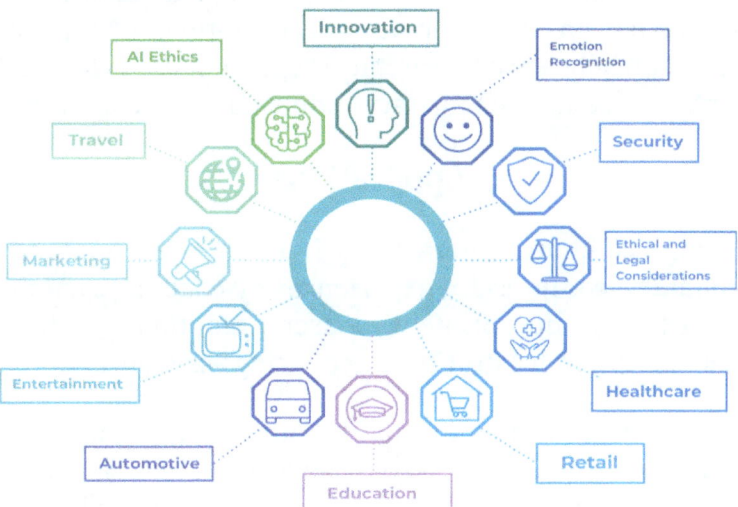

Figure 11: 12 applications of facial recognition technology

We shall now delve deeper into each topic:

Facial Emotion Recognition

Facial emotion recognition is detecting and identifying human emotions from facial expressions. It involves various techniques, applications, and challenges:

Techniques

Feature-based methods: These methods analyze specific facial features, such as the position of the eyebrows, eyes, nose, and mouth, to infer emotions. Attributes are extracted using algorithms like Gabor filters or Local Binary Patterns (LBP).

Deep learning models: Deep learning, especially Convolutional Neural Networks (CNNs), has remarkably succeeded in facial emotion recognition. CNNs can automatically learn hierarchical representations of facial features, leading to more accurate emotion recognition.

Applications

Human-computer interaction: Emotion recognition can enhance user interface experiences by enabling systems to respond appropriately to users' emotions, such as detecting user frustration and offering assistance.

Mental health monitoring: Emotion recognition can assist in monitoring and diagnosing mental health conditions such as depression and anxiety. It can help in early detection and intervention.

Market research: Emotion recognition can be used to understand consumer reactions to products, advertisements, or services. It gives valued insights into consumer preferences and behaviors.

Challenges

Variations in facial expressions: Facial expressions can vary widely across individuals, cultures, and contexts, making it challenging to develop a universal emotion recognition system.

> **13. Cultural differences:** Emotion expressions can be influenced by cultural norms and practices, leading to differences in how emotions are expressed and perceived.

Ethical considerations: There are ethical troubles related to privacy and consent when using facial emotion recognition, especially in public or sensitive settings. Ensuring data protection and user consent is crucial.

Limited labeled data: Training deep learning models for emotion recognition requires large labeled datasets, which can be challenging to obtain, especially for complex emotions or specific cultural contexts.

Facial Recognition in Security

Facial recognition in security involves using facial biometrics to identify individuals for security purposes. It encompasses various techniques, applications, and challenges:

Techniques

Feature-based methods: These methods extract facial features such as the eyes, nose, and mouth and use them to create a unique facial signature for each individual.

Deep learning models: Deep learning, particularly Convolutional Neural Networks (CNNs), has significantly advanced facial recognition accuracy in security. CNNs can learn complex patterns in facial images, improving recognition performance.

Applications

Access control: Facial recognition is used for secure access to buildings, rooms, and devices. It replaces traditional methods like keycards or passwords.

Surveillance: Facial recognition is employed in surveillance systems to monitor public spaces, airports, and other high-security areas to identify and track individuals of interest.

Forensic analysis: Law enforcement agencies use facial recognition to match faces in surveillance footage or images with criminal databases to identify suspects or missing persons.

Challenges

Accuracy and reliability: Ensuring the high accuracy and reliability of facial recognition systems is challenging, especially in varying lighting conditions, angles, and facial expressions.

Privacy concerns: There are concerns regarding the collection, storage, and use of facial biometric data, raising privacy and civil liberty issues.

Bias and fairness: Facial recognition systems can exhibit bias, leading to inaccuracies, particularly for specific demographic groups. Ensuring fairness and mitigating bias is a significant challenge.

Regulatory compliance: Adhering to regulations and standards, such as GDPR, CCPA, and others, regarding the collection and use of facial biometric data poses challenges for organizations implementing facial recognition systems.

Ethical and Legal Factors

Ethical and legal considerations are vital aspects of implementing facial recognition technology. They encompass various elements, including data privacy, bias, and regulatory compliance:

Data Privacy

Consent: Ensuring individuals' consent before collecting and using their facial biometric data is essential. Organizations must inform individuals about the purpose of data collection and obtain explicit consent.
Data protection: Safeguarding facial biometric data against unauthorized access, use, or disclosure is critical. Implementing strong security measures and encryption techniques is necessary to protect data privacy.

Bias and fairness

Algorithmic bias: Facial recognition algorithms can exhibit bias, leading to inaccuracies, particularly for specific demographic groups. Addressing discrimination requires diverse and representative training data and ongoing algorithmic audits.
Fairness: Ensuring fairness in facial recognition systems involves ensuring equal treatment and prospects for all

individuals, regardless of their demographic characteristics.

Regulatory compliance

GDPR: The General Data Protection Regulation (GDPR) in the EU regulates the processing of personal data, including facial biometric data, and imposes strict requirements for data protection and individual rights.
CCPA: The California Consumer Privacy Act (CCPA) expects organizations to disclose their data collection practices and allow consumers to opt out of selling their personal information, including facial biometric data.
Other regulations: Various other regulations and standards, such as the Biometric Information Privacy Act (BIPA) in Illinois, USA, and the Personal Information Protection Law (PIPL) in China, impose restrictions on the collection and use of facial biometric data.

Ethical considerations

Transparency: It is critical to ensure transparency in facial recognition technology, including disclosing how it works and its potential impact on individuals.
Accountability: Establishing accountability mechanisms to address facial recognition technology's misuse or unintended consequences is crucial for maintaining public trust.

Public perception and trust

Education and awareness: Educating the public about facial recognition technology, its benefits, risks, and limitations can help build trust and mitigate concerns.

Stakeholder engagement: Engaging with stakeholders, including civil society organizations, privacy advocates, and policymakers, can help address concerns and ensure the ethical use of facial recognition technology.

Facial Recognition in Healthcare

Facial recognition in healthcare involves using facial biometrics for various applications in the healthcare industry. Here's an overview of the techniques, applications, and challenges in this field:

Techniques

Facial feature extraction: Similar to other fields, facial recognition in healthcare involves extracting facial features such as eyes, nose, and mouth to establish a unique facial signature.

Deep learning models: Deep learning, particularly Convolutional Neural Networks (CNNs), is used to improve accuracy in facial recognition in healthcare. CNNs can learn complex patterns in facial images, aiding in recognition.

Applications

Patient identification: Facial recognition can be used for accurate and secure patient identification, reducing errors in medical records and ensuring correct treatment.

Emotional analysis: Facial recognition can help analyze patients' emotional states, which can be valuable for mental health assessments and *monitoring*.

Pain assessment: Facial recognition can assist in pain assessment, especially in non-verbal patients or those unable to communicate effectively.

Challenges

Privacy and security: Confirming the confidentiality and security of patients' facial biometric data is crucial to conforming with HIPAA (Health Insurance Portability and Accountability Act) regulations in the United States.

Accuracy and reliability: Facial recognition systems must be accurate and reliable, especially in healthcare settings where patient safety and well-being are paramount.

Ethical considerations: There are ethical worries related to using facial recognition in healthcare, such as consent, data protection, and potential bias in algorithms.

Facial Recognition in Retail

Facial recognition technology is progressively used in the retail industry for various purposes. Here's an overview of the techniques, applications, and challenges associated with facial recognition in retail:

Techniques

Facial feature extraction: Facial recognition systems use algorithms to detect and extract facial features such as eyes, nose, and mouth. These features are then used to create a unique facial signature for each individual.

Deep learning models: Deep learning, particularly Convolutional Neural Networks (CNNs), is commonly used for facial recognition in retail. These models can learn complex patterns in facial images, leading to more accurate recognition.

Applications

Customer profiling: Facial recognition can be used to profile customers based on their demographics, such as age, gender, and ethnicity. This information can help retailers understand their consumer base better and tailor their promotion strategies accordingly.

Personalized marketing: Retailers can use facial recognition to personalize marketing messages and customer offers. For example, a store can display customized ads or discounts based on the customer's profile.

Loss prevention: Facial recognition can help retailers identify known shoplifters or individuals with suspicious behavior. It can also be used to monitor employees and prevent internal theft.

Customer experience: Facial recognition can enhance the customer experience by enabling frictionless payments, personalized shopping experiences, and efficient customer service.

Challenges

Privacy concerns: Facial recognition raises privacy concerns, as it involves collecting and storing biometric data. Merchants must ensure that they comply with relevant privacy laws and regulations.

Accuracy and bias: Facial recognition systems may not be 100% accurate and can exhibit bias, especially against certain demographic groups. Retailers must regularly test and calibrate their systems to minimize these issues.

Regulatory compliance: Retailers using facial recognition technology must comply with regulations such as the General Data Protection Regulation (GDPR) in the EU and the California Consumer Privacy Act (CCPA) in the US, which impose strict requirements for collecting and using biometric data.

Facial Recognition in Education

Facial recognition technology is increasingly being explored for various applications in education. Here's an overview of the techniques, applications, and challenges associated with facial recognition in education:

Techniques

Facial feature extraction: Facial recognition systems use algorithms to detect and extract facial features such as eyes, nose, and mouth. These features are then used to create a unique facial signature for each individual.

Deep learning models: Deep learning, particularly Convolutional Neural Networks (CNNs), is commonly used for facial recognition in education. These models can learn complex patterns in facial images, leading to more accurate recognition.

Applications

Student identification: Facial recognition can accurately identify students, track attendance, and manage access to facilities and resources. This can help improve security and streamline administrative processes.

Personalized learning: Facial recognition can personalize learning experiences based on students' facial expressions and responses. For example, the system can adjust the difficulty level of questions or provide additional support based on the student's engagement and understanding.

Behavioral analysis: Facial recognition can be used to analyze students' behavior and emotions in the classroom. This information can help educators understand students' needs and tailor their teaching approach accordingly.

Security: Facial recognition can enhance safety on school premises by identifying unauthorized individuals and alerting security personnel.

Challenges

Privacy concerns: Facial recognition raises concerns, mainly when used with children. Schools must ensure that they have appropriate consent mechanisms and comply with relevant privacy laws and regulations.

Accuracy and bias: Facial recognition systems may not be 100% accurate and can exhibit bias, especially against certain demographic groups. Schools must regularly test and calibrate their systems to minimize these issues.

Ethical considerations: There are ethical considerations related to using facial recognition in education, such as consent, data protection, and potential misuse of the technology for surveillance purposes.

Facial Recognition in Automotive

Facial recognition technology is progressively being integrated into automotive systems for various applications. Here's an overview of the techniques, applications, and challenges associated with facial recognition in the automotive industry:

Techniques

Facial feature extraction: Facial recognition systems use algorithms to detect and extract facial features such as eyes, nose, and mouth. These features are then used to create a unique facial signature for each individual.

Deep learning models: Deep learning, particularly Convolutional Neural Networks (CNNs), is commonly used for facial recognition in automotive applications. These models can learn complex patterns in facial images, leading to more accurate recognition.

Applications

Driver monitoring: Facial recognition can monitor driver behavior, including drowsiness detection, distraction detection, and driver identification. This can help improve road safety.

Personalized driving experience: Facial recognition can personalize the driving experience, such as adjusting seat positions, climate control settings, and in-car entertainment based on the driver's preferences.

Vehicle security: Facial recognition can enhance vehicle security by identifying authorized drivers and preventing unauthorized access. It can also help in tracking stolen vehicles by identifying the thief.

Driver authentication: Facial recognition can be used for driver authentication, replacing traditional key-based or keyless entry systems.

Challenges

Accuracy and reliability: Ensuring facial recognition systems' high accuracy and reliability in varying lighting conditions, angles, and facial expressions is challenging but crucial for safety.

Privacy concerns: Facial recognition raises privacy concerns, as it involves collecting and storing biometric data. Automotive manufacturers must ensure that they comply with relevant privacy laws and regulations.

Ethical considerations: There are ethical considerations related to using facial recognition in automotive applications, such as consent, data protection, and potential misuse of the technology for surveillance purposes.

Facial Recognition in Entertainment

Facial recognition technology is increasingly used for various entertainment industry applications. Here's an overview of the techniques, applications, and challenges associated with facial recognition in entertainment:

Techniques

Facial feature extraction: Facial recognition systems use algorithms to detect and extract facial features such as eyes, nose, and mouth. These features are then used to create a unique facial signature for each individual.

Deep learning models: Deep learning, particularly Convolutional Neural Networks (CNNs), is commonly used for facial recognition in entertainment. These models can learn complex patterns in facial images, leading to more accurate recognition.

Applications

Content recommendation: Facial recognition can recommend content, such as movies, TV shows, or music, based on the viewer's facial expressions and emotional responses.

Audience analysis: Facial recognition can analyze audience demographics, engagement levels, and emotional responses during live events or performances. This information can help producers and performers tailor their content to suit their audience better.

User engagement: Facial recognition can enhance engagement with entertainment content by enabling interactive experiences, personalized recommendations, and targeted advertising.

Challenges

Accuracy and reliability: Ensuring facial recognition systems' high accuracy and reliability in capturing and interpreting facial expressions, especially in dynamic and varied environments, is crucial for practical audience analysis and content recommendation.

Privacy concerns: Facial recognition raises privacy concerns, as it involves collecting and storing biometric data. Entertainment companies must ensure that they comply with relevant privacy laws and regulations.

Ethical considerations: There are ethical considerations related to using facial recognition in entertainment, such as consent, data protection, and potential misuse of the technology for surveillance purposes.

Facial Recognition in Marketing

Facial recognition technology is progressively being utilized in marketing for various applications. Here's an overview of the techniques, applications, and challenges associated with facial recognition in marketing:

Techniques

Facial feature extraction: Facial recognition systems use algorithms to detect and extract facial features such as eyes, nose, and mouth. These features are then used to create a unique facial signature for each individual.

Deep learning models: Deep learning, particularly Convolutional Neural Networks (CNNs), is commonly used for facial recognition in marketing. These models can learn complex patterns in facial images, leading to more accurate recognition.

Applications

Customer segmentation: Facial recognition can segment customers based on their demographics, such as age, gender, and ethnicity. This information can help marketers target specific customer segments with personalized marketing campaigns.

Targeted advertising: Facial recognition can personalize advertising messages and offers for individual customers. For example, a billboard can display different commercials based on the demographics of the people passing by.

Campaign analysis: Facial recognition can be used to study the effectiveness of marketing campaigns by measuring customer engagement, emotional responses, and conversion rates.

Challenges

Privacy concerns: Facial recognition raises privacy concerns, as it involves collecting and storing biometric data. Marketers must ensure that they comply with relevant privacy laws and regulations.

Accuracy and bias: Ensuring high accuracy and minimizing bias in facial recognition systems is crucial for effective customer segmentation and targeted advertising. Marketers must regularly test and calibrate their strategies to mitigate these issues.

Ethical considerations: There are ethical considerations related to using facial recognition in marketing, such as consent, data protection, and potential misuse of the technology for intrusive advertising.

Facial Recognition in Travel

Facial recognition technology is increasingly used for various applications in the travel industry. Here's an overview of the techniques, applications, and challenges associated with facial recognition in travel:

Techniques

Facial feature extraction: Facial recognition systems use algorithms to detect and extract facial features such as eyes, nose, and mouth. These features are then used to create a unique facial signature for each individual.

Deep learning models: Deep learning, particularly Convolutional Neural Networks (CNNs), is commonly used for facial recognition in travel. These models can learn complex patterns in facial images, leading to more accurate recognition.

Applications

Customer profiling: Facial recognition can be used to profile customers based on their demographics, such as age, gender, and nationality. This information can help travel companies tailor their services to better suit their customers' preferences.

Personalized services: Facial recognition can be used to personalize travel experiences, such as hotel accommodations, transportation, and entertainment, based on the customer's preferences.

Security: Facial recognition can enhance security at airports and other travel hubs by identifying travelers and matching them with their travel documents, such as passports or boarding passes.

Challenges

Privacy concerns: Facial recognition raises privacy concerns, as it involves collecting and storing biometric data. Travel companies must ensure that they comply with relevant privacy laws and regulations.

Accuracy and reliability: Ensuring facial recognition systems' high accuracy and reliability in varying lighting conditions, angles, and facial expressions is crucial for security and customer satisfaction.

Ethical considerations: There are ethical considerations related to using facial recognition in travel, such as consent, data protection, and potential misuse of the technology for surveillance purposes.

Facial Recognition and AI Ethics

Facial recognition technology raises several ethical considerations that need to be addressed. Here's an overview of the techniques, applications, and challenges associated with facial recognition and AI ethics:

Techniques

Facial feature extraction: Facial recognition systems use algorithms to detect and extract facial features such as eyes, nose, and mouth. These features are then used to create a unique facial signature for each individual.

Deep learning models: Deep learning, particularly Convolutional Neural Networks (CNNs), is commonly used for facial recognition. These models can learn complex patterns in facial images, leading to more accurate recognition.

Applications

Surveillance: Facial recognition is used in surveillance systems for security purposes, such as identifying suspects or monitoring public spaces.

Access control: Facial recognition is used for secure access to buildings, devices, and systems, replacing traditional methods like keycards or passwords.

Marketing and advertising: Facial recognition is used in marketing and advertising to personalize messages and offers based on customer demographics.

Healthcare: Facial recognition is used for patient identification, record-keeping, and monitoring.

Challenges

Privacy concerns: Facial recognition raises privacy concerns, as it involves collecting and storing biometric data. Concerns about how this data is used, shared, and protected exist.

Bias and discrimination: Facial recognition systems can exhibit bias, leading to inaccuracies, particularly for specific demographic groups. This can result in differences and unfair treatment.

Surveillance and control: There are concerns about using facial recognition for mass observation and government control, infringing on individuals' rights to privacy and freedom.

Regulatory and legal issues: There is an absence of clear regulations and laws governing the use of facial recognition technology, leading to uncertainty and potential misuse.

Future Trends and Innovations

Future trends and innovations in facial recognition technology will likely focus on enhancing accuracy, expanding applications, and addressing ethical and privacy concerns. Here's an overview:

Techniques

Improved accuracy: Future advancements may involve refining algorithms and training models on larger, more diverse datasets to improve recognition accuracy, especially in challenging conditions like poor lighting or partial occlusions.

Multi-modal biometrics: Combining facial recognition with other biometric modalities, such as fingerprints or iris scans, to enhance security and accuracy.

Real-time processing: Faster and more efficient processing techniques to enable real-time facial recognition in various applications.

Applications

Healthcare: Enhanced facial recognition systems could assist in diagnosing medical conditions based on facial features or monitoring patient health remotely.

Retail: Personalized shopping experiences based on facial recognition could become more prevalent, with targeted offers and recommendations.

Security: Facial recognition could be used with other security measures for enhanced authentication and access control.

Education: Facial recognition could be used in classrooms to monitor student engagement and personalize learning experiences.

Challenges

Privacy concerns: As facial detection technology becomes more prevalent, there are increasing concerns about the collection, storage, and use of biometric data, requiring robust privacy protections.

Bias and fairness: Addressing discrimination in facial recognition algorithms to ensure fairness and accuracy, especially for underrepresented groups.

Regulatory and legal issues: Developing and implementing standards to regulate the use of facial detection technology to protect individuals' rights and ensure ethical use.

Security vulnerabilities: Ensuring facial recognition systems are secure against hacking and misuse, particularly in sensitive applications like financial transactions or access control.

Conclusion

Facial recognition technology has evolved significantly, driven by improvements in deep learning and computer vision algorithms. Techniques such as facial feature extraction and deep learning models, particularly Convolutional Neural Networks (CNNs), are critical to its success. These methods enable the detection and extraction of facial features, creating unique facial signatures for each individual. However, challenges such as accuracy, bias, privacy, and ethical considerations remain.

In various industries, facial recognition has found diverse applications. In security, it enhances access control and surveillance. In healthcare, it aids in patient identification and emotional analysis. In retail, it enables customer profiling and personalized marketing. In education, it assists in student identification and customized learning. In automotive, it enhances driver monitoring and security. In entertainment, it personalizes content recommendation and audience analysis. In marketing, it enables customer segmentation and targeted advertising. In travel, it helps in customer profiling and personalized services.

Despite its potential benefits, facial recognition technology raises several ethical and legal concerns. Privacy issues arise from the collection and storage of biometric data. Bias and fairness concerns arise from inaccuracies, especially against certain demographic groups. Ethical considerations include consent, data protection, and potential misuse for surveillance purposes. Regulatory compliance is crucial, with laws such as GDPR, CCPA, and others imposing strict requirements for data protection and individual rights.

Future trends and innovations in facial recognition are expected to focus on improving accuracy, expanding applications, and addressing ethical and privacy concerns. This includes improving algorithms and processing techniques, integrating multi-modal biometrics, and enhancing real-time processing capabilities. However, addressing privacy, bias, and regulatory compliance will be crucial to ensuring facial recognition technology's responsible and ethical use across industries.

Chapter 8: A Strategic Implementation Roadmap

This chapter will reveal a detailed strategic roadmap for implementing "Periocular Insights: Unravelling Age and Gender Classification - A Deep Learning Approach" across multiple industries. The roadmap outlines the methodology behind age and gender classification and explores its application's advantages and disadvantages within each sector. By examining the intricacies of this deep learning approach, readers will gain valuable insights into how advanced technology can address specific challenges and seize emerging opportunities. This chapter aims to provide readers with the knowledge and understanding required to implement age and gender effectively.

Figure 12: 10 implications for further advancement

classification solutions across diverse domains.

1. **Retail**

    ➢ **Strategy**: Implement facial recognition cameras at store entrances and analyze customer demographics in real time. Use this data for targeted marketing campaigns and optimizing store layouts.

- **Pros**: Personalized shopping experience, targeted marketing, optimized store layouts.
- **Cons**: Privacy concerns, data security issues, and potential customer backlash.

2. *Healthcare*

- **Strategy**: Integrate facial recognition technology into patient monitoring systems. Use the data for personalized treatment plans and patient identification.
- **Pros**: Improved patient care, personalized treatment plans, and efficient identification.
- **Cons**: Privacy concerns, regulatory compliance issues, potential bias in treatment plans.

3. *Marketing*

- **Strategy**: Use facial recognition technology to analyze customer demographics in real time. Tailor marketing campaigns and product recommendations based on the analysis.
- **Pros**: Targeted advertising, improved campaign effectiveness, personalized product recommendations.
- **Cons**: Privacy concerns, data security issues, and potential customer backlash.

4. *Entertainment*

- **Strategy**: Implement facial recognition technology in content recommendation systems: Personalize movie, TV show, and music recommendations based on the viewer's age and gender.

- **Pros**: Enhanced user experience, increased viewer engagement, improved content discovery.

- **Cons**: Privacy concerns, potential bias in content recommendations, and data security issues.

5. Hospitality

- **Strategy**: Use facial recognition technology for guest profiling. Offer personalized services and room amenities based on the guest's age and gender.

- **Pros**: Enhanced guest experience, personalized services, improved customer satisfaction.

- **Cons**: Privacy concerns, data security issues, and potential guest backlash.

6. Automotive

- **Strategy**: Implement facial recognition technology for driver monitoring. Personalize in-car experiences based on the driver's age and gender.

- **Pros**: Improved driver safety, personalized driving experiences, enhanced vehicle security.

- **Cons**: Privacy concerns, data security issues, potential driver distraction.

7. *Financial Services*

   ➢ **Strategy**: Use facial recognition technology for customer profiling. Offer personalized financial advice and services based on the customer's age and gender.

   ➢ **Pros**: Improved customer satisfaction, personalized financial solutions, enhanced security.

   ➢ **Cons**: Privacy concerns, data security issues, potential bias in financial advice.

8. *Education*

   ➢ **Strategy**: Implement facial recognition technology for student profiling: Personalize learning plans and educational content based on the student's age and gender.

   ➢ **Pros**: Improved student engagement, personalized learning experiences, and enhanced educational outcomes.

   ➢ **Cons**: Privacy concerns, data security issues, and potential bias in educational content.

9. *Security*

   ➢ **Strategy**: Use facial recognition technology for access control and surveillance. Improve security measures based on the analysis of age and gender demographics.

   ➢ **Pros**: Enhanced security, improved surveillance capabilities, faster response times.

- **Cons**: Privacy concerns, data security issues, potential misuse of surveillance data.

10. Travel

- **Strategy**: Use facial recognition technology for customer profiling in travel agencies. Offer personalized travel recommendations and services based on the customer's age and gender.

- **Pros**: Enhanced customer experience, personalized travel plans, and improved customer satisfaction.

- **Cons**: Privacy concerns, data security issues, potential bias in travel recommendations.

While implementing "Periocular Insights" can offer numerous benefits, such as personalized experiences and improved customer satisfaction, it's essential to address privacy concerns, data security issues, and potential technological biases to ensure successful implementation and acceptance in each industry.

Field	Pros	Cons
Retail	Personalized shopping experience, targeted marketing, optimized store layouts	Privacy concerns, data security issues, and potential customer backlash.
Healthcare	Improved patient care, personalized treatment plans, and efficient identification.	Privacy concerns, regulatory compliance issues, potential bias in treatment plans.
Marketing	Targeted advertising, improved campaign effectiveness, personalized product recommendations.	Privacy concerns, data security issues, and potential customer backlash.
Entertainment	Enhanced user experience, increased viewer engagement, improved content discovery.	Privacy concerns, potential bias in content recommendations, and data security issues.
Hospitality	Enhanced guest experience, personalized services, improved customer satisfaction.	Privacy concerns, data security issues, and potential guest backlash.
Automotive	Improved driver safety, personalized driving experiences, enhanced vehicle security.	Privacy concerns, data security issues, potential driver distraction.
Financial Services	Improved customer satisfaction, personalized financial solutions, enhanced security.	Privacy concerns, data security issues, potential bias in financial advice.
Education	Improved student engagement, personalized learning experiences, enhanced educational outcomes.	Privacy concerns, data security issues, potential bias in educational content.
Security	Enhanced security, improved surveillance capabilities, faster response times.	Privacy concerns, data security issues, potential misuse of surveillance data.
Travel	Enhanced customer experience, personalized travel plans, and improved customer satisfaction.	Privacy concerns, data security issues, potential bias in travel recommendations.

Table 3: Pros and Cons of each field,

Conclusion

In the culminating chapter of this comprehensive exploration, I distill the collective knowledge and insights gleaned from our meticulous investigation into Periocular Age and Gender Recognition. This concluding discourse encapsulates a synthesis of our findings, shedding light on the unique attributes and challenges encountered throughout the journey.

Summary of Findings and Insights

Our endeavors have unearthed significant findings in the realms of Age and gender classification within the periocular domain. A comprehensive overview distills these discoveries, offering a panoramic view of our research's discerned patterns, model performances, and practical implications. This section crystallizes the essence of our contributions, providing readers with a complete overview of the knowledge derived from our investigations. Through detailed analysis, readers gain insights into the nuances of periocular features, model performances, and the broader implications for Age and gender recognition.

Limitations and Future Directions

Acknowledging the imperfections inherent in any scientific inquiry, we transparently delineate the boundaries encountered in our study. By doing so, we pave the way for future researchers to build upon our work, offering a critical foundation for further exploration. In addition, we outline potential avenues for future research directions, envisioning a roadmap for the continual evolution of Periocular Age and Gender Recognition technologies. This section invites readers to critically assess the limitations of our study while inspiring the pursuit of future advancements in the field.

Significance of Periocular Age and Gender Recognition

The ultimate significance of our research lies in its capacity to reshape the landscape of facial recognition technologies. By focusing on the periocular region, our work contributes not only to the advancement of accurate Age and gender classification but also underscores the broader implications for applications in security, healthcare, and human-computer interaction. This section articulates the lasting impact of our study and its potential to influence technological advancements in diverse domains. Readers are encouraged to reflect on the transformative potential of Periocular Age and Gender Recognition in focusing on real-world challenges and shaping the future of facial recognition technologies.

This chapter serves as a comprehensive synthesis, distilling the essence of our exploration and providing readers with a nuanced understanding of the implications, limitations, and significance of Periocular Age and Gender Recognition. In this project, we wanted to classify periocular images based on gender and Age. One of the ways to boost the advancements of computer vision techniques is to make the model robust. It must be able to detect and correctly identify the images even though various and unavoidable occlusions obscure the image. The fact that we use periocular images for classification already makes this a challenging one, but it does not hinder the performance. In the case of GC, it even outperforms classical models reliant on the entire face for data. Since the world is still reeling from the pandemic's effects, this project is instrumental because of the high availability of periocular images and the lack of regular photos. We implemented a Peri Gender model that utilizes skip connections and residual blocks. The performance of this model was then documented, analyzed, and compared to a few pre-trained ResNet models, namely ResNet-18, ResNet-34, and ResNet-50. After this, we modified the Peri gender model to give us predictions for age intervals. This was also evaluated alongside the ResNet mentioned above models.

Chapter 9: References

1. C. B. Ng, Y. H. Tay, and B. M. Goi, "A review of facial gender recognition," Pattern Analysis and Applications, vol. 18, no. 4, pp. 739-755, 2015.

2. Wu, Wenying, et al. "Gender classification and bias mitigation in facial images." 12th ACM conference on web science. 2020.

3. S. S. Liew, M. K. Hani, S. A. Radzi and R. Bakhteri, "Gender classification: A convolutional neural network approach," Turkish Journal of Electrical Engineering & Computer Sciences, vol. 24, no. 3, pp. 1248-1264, 2016.

4. M. Ngan and P. Grother, "Face recognition vendor test (FRVT) performance of automated gender classification algorithms," US Department of Commerce, National Institute of Standards and Technology, NISTIR 8271, 186, 2015 https://doi.org/10.6028/NIST.IR.8271.

5. F. A. Fernandez and J. Bigun, "A survey on periocular biometrics research," Pattern Recognition Letters, vol. 82, no. 2, pp. 92-105, 201

6. D. Bobeldyk and A. Ross, "Iris or periocular? Exploring sex prediction from near-infrared ocular images," in Int. Conf. of the Biometrics Special Interest Group (BIOSIG), Darmstadt, Germany, 2016.

7. E. Brown and D. I. Perrett, "What gives a face its gender," Perception, vol. 22, no. 7, pp. 829-840, 1993.

8. F. J. Xu, E. Verma, P. Goel, A. Cherodian and M. Savvides, "Deep Gender: Occlusion and low-resolution robust facial gender classification via progressively trained convolutional neural networks with attention," in Proc. of the IEEE Conf. on Computer Vision and Pattern Recognition Workshops, Las Vegas, NV, USA, 2016.

9. R. Alrabiah, M. Hussain, and H. A. AboAlSamh, "Unconstrained Gender Recognition from Periocular Region Using Multiscale Deep Features," Intelligent Automation & Soft Computing, vol. 35, no. 3, pp. 2941-2962, 2023, Doi: 10.32604/iasc.2023.030036.

10. Pablo Barros and Alessandra Sciutti, 'I Only Have Eyes for You: The Impact of Masks on Convolutional-Based Facial Expression Recognition, arXiv:2104.08353v1 [cs.CV] 16 Apr 2021

11. Yaaseen Muhammad Saib, Sameer Chand Pudaruth, 'Is Face Recognition with Masks Possible?' in International Journal of Advanced Computer Science and Applications, Vol.12, No. 7, 202, 43-50

12. Bishwas Mandal, Adaeze Okeukwu, Yihong Theis, 'Masked Face Recognition using ResNet-50', arXiv:2104.08997v1 [cs.CV], 2021.

13. Pedro C. Neto et al., 'My Eyes Are Up Here: Promoting Focus on Uncovered Regions in Masked Face Recognition,' arXiv:2108.00996v3 [cs.CV] 18 Aug 2021

14. Yaaseen Muhammad Saib, Sameer Chand Pudaruth, 'Is Face Recognition with Masks Possible?' in International Journal of Advanced Computer Science and Applications, Vol. 12, No. 7, 2021 43-50

15. Chandrashekhar Padole, Hugo Proença; Periocular Recognition: Analysis of Performance Degradation Factors, in Proceedings of the Fifth IAPR/IEEE International Conference on Biometrics – ICB 2012, New Delhi, India, March 30-April 1, 2012.

16. Beautiful Free Images & Pictures, Unsplashed, 2021. [Online]. Available: https://unsplash.com/.

17. Free stock photos, royalty-free stock images, Pixels, 2021. [Online]. Available: https://www.pexels.com/.

18. F. H. B. Zavan, O. R. P. Bellon, L. Silva, and G. G. Medioni, "Benchmarking parts-based face processing in the wild for gender recognition and head pose estimation," Pattern Recognition Letters, vol. 123, no. 1, pp. 104–110, 2019.

19. Dhomne, R. Kumar and V. Bhan, "Gender recognition through face using deep learning," Procedia Computer Science, vol. 132, no. 1, pp. 2–10, 2018.

20. M. C. Santana, J. L. Navarro, and E. R. Balmaseda, "Descriptors and regions of interest fusion for in- and cross-database gender classification in the wild," Image and Vision Computing, vol. 57, no. 1, pp. 15–24, 2017.

21. Bisogni, Carmen & Cascone, Lucia & Narducci, Fabio. (2022). Periocular Data Fusion for Age and Gender Classification. Journal of Imaging. 8. 307. 10.3390/jimaging8110307.

22. arXiv:1901.07884v7

23. Yanwei Fu, Timothy M. Hospedales, Tao Xiang, Jiechao Xiong, Shaogang Gong, Yizhou Wang, and Yuan Yao. Robust Subjective Visual Property Prediction from Crowdsourced Pairwise Labels. IEEE TPAMI 2016

24. Zhang, Z., Song, Y., Qi, H., Ma, Y. UTK Face Dataset. 2017. [Online]. Available - https://susanqq.github.io/UTKFace/

25. Wang, Z. J., Turko, R., Shaikh, O., Park, H., Das, N., Hohman, F., Kahng, M., & Chau, D. H. (2020). CNN Explainer: Learning Convolutional Neural Networks with Interactive Visualization. IEEE Transactions on Visualization and Computer Graphics (TVCG). Retrieved from [https://poloclub.github.io/cnn-explainer/]

26. Basista, A. (2021). Face Detection Repository. GitHub. https://github.com/basista21/face-detection

Chapter 10: Glossary

1. **Computer Vision**: A field of artificial intelligence and computer science that focuses on enabling computers to interpret and understand the visual world, including images and videos.

2. **Model**: In machine learning and artificial intelligence, a model refers to a mathematical representation or computational algorithm that learns patterns and relationships from data to make predictions, classifications, or decisions.

3. **Periocular**: Refers to the region surrounding the eyes, including the eyebrows and eyes.

4. **Training**: Training refers to teaching a model to make predictions or perform a specific task by exposing it to a dataset containing labeled examples.

5. **Testing**: testing refers to the evaluation phase where the performance of a trained model is assessed using unseen data to measure its accuracy, generalization capability, and robustness.

6. **Transformations**: Transformations refer to altering or modifying data from one representation to another, often to improve its usability, interpretability, or performance in a machine-learning context.

7. **Age and Gender Recognition**: The process of identifying and categorizing individuals based on

their age and gender using computational methods, often within the context of computer vision.

8. **Facial Recognition**: A biometric technology that analyses facial features to verify or identify individuals.

9. **Soft Biometric Traits**: Characteristics such as ethnicity, gender, and approximate age that can be inferred from an individual's appearance.

10. **Convolutional Neural Networks (CNNs)**: A deep learning algorithm commonly used in computer vision tasks for processing and analyzing visual data.

11. **Gender Classification (GC)**: The task of categorizing individuals into distinct gender categories based on visual cues or features.

12. **Datasets**: These are data collections used for training and testing machine learning algorithms, including those related to facial recognition and computer vision tasks.

13. **Occlusions**: Obstructions or coverings that wholly or partially obscure parts of an object or image, such as masks or other facial coverings.

14. **Real-world Scenarios**: Practical situations or environments where technologies such as periocular age and gender recognition may be applied, including security, surveillance, and marketing.

15. **Convolutional Neural Networks (CNNs)**: A class of deep neural networks commonly applied to analyzing visual imagery.

16. **Iris Recognition**: A biometric identification method that utilizes the unique patterns in the eye's iris for recognition.

17. **Discriminative Information**: Features or characteristics beneficial for distinguishing between different classes or categories, such as gender.

18. **Invasive Approach**: Techniques or methods that require physical contact or intrusion into the body, such as using the iris for gender classification, which may not be socially acceptable or suitable for unconstrained scenarios.

19. **Topography of Computer Vision**: The landscape or terrain of the field of computer vision, which is characterized by ongoing innovation and development.

20. **Transformative Exploration**: A journey of discovery and investigation to bring about significant changes or advancements, as exemplified by the pioneering exploration into periocular age and gender recognition described in the text.

21. **Masked Facial Recognition**: The capability of recognizing individuals even when masks or other obstructions partially cover their faces.

22. **Occlusions**: Obstructions or coverings that partially or entirely obscure parts of an object or image, such as masks or other facial coverings.

23. **Periocular Region**: The area surrounding the eyes, including the eyebrows and corners of the eyes.

24. **Data Augmentation**: Techniques used to artificially increase the size of a dataset by applying various transformations to the existing data, such as rotation, flipping, or cropping.

25. **ResNet Models**: A family of deep neural network models known for their residual learning framework, commonly used in image recognition tasks.

26. **Baseline Model**: A simple model or method used as a benchmark for comparison with more complex or advanced models.

27. **Preprocessing**: The manipulation and transformation of raw data into a format suitable for analysis or machine learning algorithms.

28. **Cross Entropy Loss**: A loss function commonly used in classification tasks, measuring the difference between predicted and actual class probabilities.

29. **Hyperparameter**: A hyperparameter is a configuration setting external to the model that influences the learning process and model architecture, impacting the performance and

behavior of the algorithm. It can be changed accordingly during the training process.

30. **Loss Function**: A loss function is a mathematical function that quantifies the discrepancy between the predicted output of a machine learning model and the actual ground truth labels or values.

31. **Learning Rate**: A hyperparameter that controls the step size during the optimization process of training a machine learning model.

32. **Momentum**: A hyperparameter that accelerates the optimization process by adding a fraction of the previous update to the current update.

33. **SGDM Optimizer**: Stochastic Gradient Descent with Momentum, an optimization algorithm commonly used in training neural networks.

34. **Activation Function**: A function applied to the output of each neuron in a neural network, determining its production based on the input.

35. **Binary Classification**: A classification task that aims to categorize data into one of two classes or categories.

36. **Confusion Matrix**: A table used to evaluate the performance of a classification model, showing the counts of true positive, true negative, false positive, and false pessimistic predictions.

37. **Data Imbalance**: A situation where one class or category in a dataset is significantly more prevalent than others, leading to biased model performance.

38. **Validation Dataset**: A subset of the dataset used to evaluate the performance of a trained machine learning model, typically not seen during training.

39. **Periocular Domain**: The specific area surrounding the eyes, including the eyebrows and corners of the eyes, is often studied in the context of facial recognition and age prediction.

40. **Age Prediction**: The process of estimating or predicting an individual's age based on various features, often within the context of computer vision and machine learning.

41. **UTK Face Dataset**: A large-scale face dataset containing over 20,000 images with annotations of age, gender, and ethnicity, commonly used for tasks such as face recognition, age estimation, and landmark localization.

42. **Age Ranges**: Categories or intervals used to represent the age of individuals, often divided into distinct ranges to capture the variability in age-related facial features.

43. **ResNet Models**: A family of deep neural network models known for their residual learning framework, commonly used in image recognition tasks.

44. **Fully Connected Layer**: A layer in a neural network where each neuron is connected to every neuron in the previous and subsequent layers, often used for classification tasks.

45. **SoftMax**: A mathematical function that converts a vector of arbitrary actual values into a probability distribution, commonly used in multi-class classification problems.

46. **FG-Net Dataset**: A dataset used for age estimation and face recognition across ages, consisting of pictures of individuals spanning a wide age range, commonly used for training and testing age prediction models.

47. **Image Resolution**: The clarity and detail present in an image, often measured in pixels, can affect machine learning models' performance.

48. **Peri Age Model**: A custom model explicitly designed for age prediction within the periocular domain, often tailored to accommodate the unique characteristics of periocular features.

49. **Data Augmentation**: Techniques used to artificially increase the size or diversity of a dataset by applying transformations such as rotation, cropping, or flipping to existing data.

50. **Arg Max**: A function that returns the indices of the maximum value along an axis, commonly used in classification tasks to determine the predicted class.

51. **Challenges in Age Prediction**: Difficulties or obstacles encountered in accurately predicting age, such as the lack of dedicated periocular datasets with pre-assigned age labels and issues with image resolution.

52. **Periocular Features**: Characteristics or attributes present in the area surrounding the eyes, often used as cues for tasks such as age prediction and gender classification.

53. **Gender Classification**: The process of categorizing individuals into distinct gender categories based on visual cues or features, often within the context of computer vision.

54. **Video Frames**: Individual images that collectively form a video sequence, each representing a specific moment in time.

55. **Face Detection**: Locating and identifying human faces within images or video frames.

56. **Temporal Dimension**: Time within a dataset or analysis, particularly relevant when considering changes or patterns over time.

57. **Real-Time**: Processing or analysis performed immediately as data becomes available, without significant delay.

58. **Algorithm**: A set of step-by-step instructions or procedures for solving a problem or completing a task, often implemented in software or computer programs.

59. **Granular Analysis**: A detailed examination or study of a subject, focusing on individual components or aspects.

60. **Facial Attributes**: Characteristics or features present on a person's face, such as gender, age, expression, and ethnicity.

61. **Synthesis**: Combining or integrating different elements or components to create a new whole.

62. **OpenCV**: Open-Source Computer Vision Library, a famous open-source computer vision and machine learning software library.

63. **Peri Gender**: A convolutional neural network architecture designed for image classification tasks, mainly focused on gender classification within the periocular domain.

64. **Residual Groups**: Components of the Peri Gender architecture denoted as Res_Gi (F, C), consisting of multiple residual blocks to enhance feature representation for gender classification.

65. **Residual Blocks**: Components of the Peri Gender architecture denoted as Res_Bj (F, C), containing convolutional layers, batch normalization, and ReLU activation functions, aiding in mitigating vanishing gradient problems in deep networks.

66. **Skip Connections**: Specialized layers in the Peri Gender architecture facilitate information propagation without transformation, preserving spatial information and aiding in feature fusion.

67. **Multiscale Features**: Features extracted at multiple scales or resolutions, fused through skip connections and depth concatenation layers in the Peri Gender architecture to enhance gender classification.

68. **Batch Normalization**: A technique that standardizes activations across mini-batches in

deep learning models, improving training efficiency and performance.

69. **ReLU Activation Function**: Rectified Linear Unit activation function introduces non-linearity into the model, widely used in deep learning architectures.

70. **Concatenation Layer**: A layer in the Peri Gender architecture combining features extracted from various sources through concatenation along the channel dimension.

71. **Activation Function**: An activation function, in the context of artificial neural networks, is a mathematical function applied to the output of each neuron, determining whether the neuron should be activated based on the input it receives.

72. **Average Pooling Layer**: A layer in the Peri Gender architecture computing the mean value within local regions to reduce dimensionality before passing data to fully connected layers.

73. **Fully Connected Layer**: The final layer in the Peri Gender architecture is responsible for binary classification (male or female) based on the extracted features, often followed by SoftMax activation.

74. **Model Deployment**: The process of making machine learning models available for use in real-world applications, typically involving the creation of user-friendly interfaces for interaction.

75. **Interactive Interface**: A user interface allowing users to interact with machine learning models, often featuring input fields for data and displaying model predictions in real time.

76. **Gradio Library**: A library used for building interactive machine learning applications, providing tools for creating user-friendly interfaces effortlessly.

77. **Predictive Prowess**: The ability of a machine learning model to accurately predict outcomes based on input data, showcased through interactive interfaces for users to leverage.

78. **Democratization of AI**: Making advanced AI technologies accessible to a wide range of users, irrespective of technical expertise, through intuitive interfaces and simplified deployment workflows.

www.ingramcontent.com/pod-product-compliance
Lightning Source LLC
Chambersburg PA
CBHW070200230526
45471CB00002B/743